My Thoughts are Complicated but the Path is Clear

About Life About Death About Last Night

Dawood Thomas

My Thoughts are Complicated but the Path is Clear

About Life About Death
About Last Night

My Thoughts are Complicated but the Path is Clear
Artwork By: Betty Dennis-Wyles
Book Design: Mikea Hugley
Texture By: Siobhan Vicens
Editor: Valencia D. Clay
ISBN: 978-0-692-90076-5

Baltimore, MD
2017

This book is dedicated to Mary Bell, Charles Thomas (RIP), Dana Baird, Charles Tia and Alicia Thomas, Tineria and Aiyana Thomas, Teione and Daisha Carroll, Stephon Reed and Ashley Kelly.... Family

Poems

About Life

After I Had Children

After I had children my social life changed,
No more hanging out all night doing strange,
Things with my friends, they don't call me as much,
I'm too busy anyway, blowing noses and wiping butts...
I use to have sex 3 or 4 times a week,
Now I'm lucky if once a week I get a peep,
Show from my wife while my daughter is sleep,
She's right in between us and hogging the sheets,
I need a relief, maybe I'll smoke a leaf,
I can't tell my wife, could this be my life?
I love my children and the life that we're building,
My son reminds me of me,
At times I be feeling,
Tired...so damn tired!
I use to play sports, I use to be in shape,
Seems it's never enough time with so much on my plate,
Can I make space, can others relate?
A great dad/alcoholic, will that be my fate?
I play little games with ulterior motives,
Hide and seek to sneak naps,
Figured out by my oldest,
Will they ever grow up?
Will they ever leave home?
Can I stay in each moment?
Can't wait until they're grown,
By then I'll be old, won't want to have sex,
Won't want to get high,
Won't care what comes next...
Now don't get me wrong,
I love the life that we're building,
But everything changed after I had children...

I'll Talk to Her in the Morning

So much to say to her, I'll start off with breakfast,
She avoided me all weekend, so passive aggressive,
I've noticed, lately we talk less and less,
I've so much on my mind, it's hard to suppress,
She said she'd been stressing too,
Said at times, she's overwhelmed,
I keep most things to myself, since I'm at the helm,
Of this ship, her and me, one accord, nothings forced,
I tell her that everything's fine, though were drifting off course...
I'm afraid because I'm nearly the age of my father when he passed,
She's afraid of mediocrity, I miss how she laughs,
In the morning I'll say, "Do you want your eggs scrambled",
She may not be ready to talk to me but, I'll take that gamble...
See...she's such a big deal to me, she's how I measure myself,
Without her, don't know how I would communicate with everyone else,
She sets the standard for me,
Though at times, I'm glad when she's gone,
Then I miss her when she's gone,
She never stays gone too long...
In the morning I'll say, "You look beautiful today",
She'll probably say thanks, eat her food, and then be on her way,
Then I'll watch her leave, watching her facial expressions,
Maybe she wants a ride but she won't ask me that question,
So I'll offer...
I'll take you to school if you don't mind,
Hoping she doesn't mind so we can have more time,
To talk...
She's so much like me that it's scary,
Picking and choosing the timing, it varies,
We haven't said more than 10 words to each other all weekend,
She's a little upset with me and that's OK,
She's 15, we have plenty of time... (God willing)
I'll just talk to her in the morning...

Emancipation

Supermarket, cook, laundry,
Why didn't y'all wash the dishes?
We in this thing together
A single fathers wishes...
My girls are so big now, my youngest even working,
My oldest ripping and running,
At least she's not out here twerking...
Or maybe she is and she has respect for me,
I know she's not a saint,
But she never let me see...

Supermarket, cook, laundry,
Now I just cleaned downstairs,
The nerve of these two,
In their rooms like they don't care...
I should make their asses clean up,
But naw, that's not my style, cleaning the house should be intrinsic,
Growth, that takes a while...

Supermarket, cook, laundry,
Her mom said, she gets no credit,
I said, let her live with you,
She made me mad,
but I aint sweat it...
I never received child support, I never went downtown,
I never regulated visitation,
And I never put their mothers down...
I did what I'm supposed to do,

Never for the praise,
Never for the accolades,
These girls done caused me greys...
I can't wait until she go back to school,
and my youngest goes over her moms,
So I can cook breakfast naked,
This shit aint just a rhyme...

Supermarket, cook, laundry,
I'm venting my frustrations,
I love my daughters,
But damn! I'm patiently waiting for their
emancipation...

4 More Years

Am I spending enough quality time with her?
She so easily swayed,
9th grade, City Knight, but so easily played,
Had to take her phone,
Made a call to her moms,
In my bedroom alone,
I resort to my rhymes...
To be a single parent,
A father in fact,
A woman wouldn't understand,
A father's impact,
Unless she had one...
My young one, makes me so upset,
Her choices are hormonal,
She doesn't see the effect,
Doesn't see it affects,
Everyone in her circle,
Don't understand, "you don't know that young man"
He could hurt you,
Then I'd have to hurt him,
Which hurts me and him,
2 birds with one stone,
Hello Satan, come in...

My young Princess,
I'm so mad right now,
I'm going to write this quick poem,
Then go lay my ass down,
Before I be on the news,
On some Adrian Peterson shit,
Frustration can get the best of me,
My response is to hit,
Or smack, or whip ass,
Whichever one fits,
But that's not always best,
I'm the first to admit...
Sisters got it hard being a single mother,
Being a single father is even harder,
Because nobody feels your pain,
And you have to move smarter,
Especially raising girls,
They're going to push a man's patience,
I reflect on my pops,
Then I stick to the basics...
It's just a behavior,
She'll grow and she'll learn,
All the shit I put my mom through,
I guess it's my turn...

"Hey Momma"

Grocery shopping on Saturdays, you always took me,
couldn't keep my hands off stuff, you always shook me,
not realizing, that I was learning skills,
now I grocery shop with my girls,
reflections so real...
my father was the best, but he was in and out,
you showed consistency with me, help me see,
what parenting's about...
a couple years we weren't close,
I was mad at you,
was really mad cause my pops wasn't there,
so I rebelled against the person,
that had always been there,
backwards thinking moms, my teenage years,
moving forward...
my siblings always said I was your favorite,
I got away with things, some was kind of flagrant...
I was such an asshole in primary grades,
days you had to take off work, days you aint get paid...
you use to whip my ass, a temporary fix,
couple days later, right back to old tricks...
caused you so much pain, not realizing at the time,
you always had my back, I was out my freaking mind...
then I starting chasing, paper was the game,
sex, drugs, violence, your son was chasing fame...
I can just imagine, the worries that I caused,
want to say I'm sorry moms, it's scary when I pause,
and think about my girls,

if they was in the streets,
can't comprehend how your strength, runs so deep,
deep inside of me, we share characteristics,,
we're more alike than different, now I feel the distance,
if I don't come and visit...
home cooked meals, your cooking is exquisite,
I've inherited some skills...
I cook now and then,
female friends be surprised,
always stayed punished, when you cooked, I applied,
everything I saw you do, sometimes you let me help,
until I got on your nerves, then, the mention of that belt,
Got my attention,
proud of you mama, even through my drama,
you taught principles and honor...
always show respect, but say what's on your mind,
taught me so much, I make the lessons rhyme...
you always showed strength, even when you cried,
told me that you loved me, even when I lied,
don't know how you put up with me,
and kept all your sanity,
some of my behaviors, were deep rooted vanity,
guess you saw a man in me,
thank you for your patience, thank you for your prayers,
thank you for the basics,
food, clothing, shelter, always provided that,
mentally a pelter, flipping words into facts,
still trying to impress you, with my fancy word play,
you're the Queen of words bae, I know I'm not worthy,
early morning Saturday,
thinking about you moms,
since you're on my mind,
you're the feature in this rhyme,
you're the feature all the time...

Real Fathers

This going out to real fathers, props to real pops, hugging the blocks, hack cocked, running shop...Get yours, ignore all the hating, make it home, your seeds waiting...
This going out to real fathers, props to real pops, pushing the mop, entrepreneur, or into stocks...a better life envisioned and created, cause the street life is overrated...
Real fathers know their kids teachers names,
If they play high school sports,
You never miss a game,
Fixing breakfast in the morning,
Just to start the day,
Conversations about god,
Asking did they pray...
Put your foot down firm,
When they gotta learn,
Always open for discussion,
When its knowledge yearned,
Even help your kids' mother,
Though she has another,
Respect that man,
Understand that he's still your brother...
When your kids live with you,
You know what to do,
No excuse, you adjust, it aint nothing new...
Your kids' mother trying to stop your visitation rights,
Put on your mental boxing gloves,
Cause it's time to fight,
You're a family man now,
Cause you've seen the light,
You got a wife,
Just look at how you changed your life,
made it right,
Sometimes I think about my father's plight,

I broke the cycle,
Took everything he taught,
To a higher height,
This going out to real fathers, props to real pops, hugging the blocks,
hack cocked, running shop...Get yours, ignore all the hating, make it
home, your seeds waiting...
This going out to real fathers, props to real pops, pushing the mop, en-
trepreneur, or into stocks...a better life envisioned and created, cause the
street life is overrated...
Real fathers got insurance policies,
When you die your seeds get at least 50 g's,
When you cry,
You aint afraid to let your children see,
You encourage them to be who they want to be...
You teach them how a choice is a power move,
Show them how to use the power,
Without breaking rules...
Tell them stand for their beliefs,
Or fall for anything,
When they fall, dust them off,
Get back in the ring,
My daughter said, "I don't want to work, I want to sing",
Now it's my job to make sure that she get seen,
I set the stage,
Now all she gotta do is dream,
I show her god,
Through me practicing my dean,
It's kinda hard sometimes,
Trying to raise a teen,
Cause the worlds so fucked up,
And they know everything,
Just be consistent,
It helps when you have a team,
You keep them fresh,
So they never have to serve the fiends,

If raising girls,
Gotta teach them about that self-esteem,
Don't be a bad bitch honey,
You can be a queen,
Yeah I mean...
This going out to real fathers, props to real pops, hugging the blocks, hack cocked, running shop...Get yours, ignore all the hating, make it home, your seeds waiting...
This going out to real fathers, props to real pops, pushing the mop, entrepreneur, or into stocks...a better life envisioned and created, cause the street life is overrated...
Real fathers, I'm thinking about a better job,
A single parent, sometimes this shit is hard,
I wanna cry, I wanna yell, or maybe fly away,
I'm overwhelmed, I sit still, time to pray,
It's hard for men to express pain to other men,
So instead we self-destruct,
While giving in to sin,
We don't think about our seeds until we in the pen,
Now we pen pals,
First line is how you been...
We realize how a choice has a great effect,
I'm careful with my words,
My girls will interject,
I don't bring no women around,
Cause I got respect,
For what they see,
Only meet the friends that I select,
Never received child support,
Wish I got a check,
Thanks to my moms and my sisters,
Cause they always kept,
Both of my girls when I'm stressed,

And I need a break,
My older and my little brother,
Both of them relate,
I can't complain,
Fatherhood helped me clean a slate,
For the way I treated women,
Probably changed my fate...
Being a father I must say,
Has changed my life,
Gave me insight,
It's a struggle but I'm doing right,
So I write...

Unconditional Love

Tineria and Aiyana,
You have no idea how you've impacted my life,
How you've challenged and changed my views on so many levels...
The way I've learned to treat woman is a direct reflection of being your father,
Believing the world is karma...
This poem isn't about rhyming and whit,
It's about gut honesty...

My girls
Tineria and Aiyana,
Who would I be without you?
Where would I be?
What would I strive for?
God had a plan that I surely didn't see,
It's an honor to help you grow into the women you'll be,
I wish my dad had the pleasure of meeting you...

My girls
Tineria and Aiyana,
Sometimes y'all drive me crazy,
And I wish I wasn't a parent...
Wished I could just run away and be free of responsibility,
Then I come around and realize,
It was never about me,
You didn't ask to be here,
But I'm glad you are,
Your life was a gift, at times I lost sight of that...

My girls
Tineria and Aiyana,
I love you with all my heart,
Thank you for allowing me to be your dad...
Unconditional love

About Death

Space

Will I ever get married?
Sometimes I say yes,
but the first time was a mess,
And I'd hate to second guess...
At times it's so lonely, I can't be phony,
But other times it's so peaceful,
A woman's tongue is so lethal,
But her touch can be the equal of massage therapy with a happy ending,
And I hope I'm not offending,
The queens that's single cause I still like to mingle,
Though I'm ready for commitment,
My heart is packaged up like a shipment,
With only a return address,
The ones I pick don't pick me back,
Do she see my best?
Growing content with being single,
Maybe get a girlfriend, be her Mandingo,
For now, until the world end...
But is that realistic?
Met a young queen I would marry but she distant,
Had a few options but I was resistant,
One I let get away, I wasn't persistent...
If you never lost love,
You've never loved at all,
You can't fall in love if you're focused on the fall,
One day I'll be ready,
Until then I'll just browse,
Built up frustrations, released through a smile...
Sending up my prayers,

Not asking for a wife,
Just a true friend I can trust with my life,
Trust with my fears, hold her close at night,
Trust with my tears, tell her that she's right,
Even when she's wrong,
We're going to be the truth,
Arguments won't last long,
Happiness is proof...
Happiness the root,
Searching for my happy place,
Drinking Absolut,
But I never drink it straight,
Add a little chase,
But this not a race,
Forget saving face,
When it's time I'll make space,
In my heart I'll make space...

"IJS"

I'm a little upset and I'll tell you why,
Because we'd rather complain and knock people that try,
We minding our own business while we watch others die,
Quick to say what we need,
but won't put money to seeds,
Grass roots organizations,
but we investing in weed,
We invest in the drinks,
that won't help our kids think...
I get it, you need a release,
but get mad at police,
for putting up with your dumb ass,
acting a fool in the streets,
Shouting about equal rights,
dude, you 40 selling pills,
Pants hanging off your ass,
claiming you keep it so real...
It's men and women in these streets advocating for change,
With their time, with their money, cause they're thinking long range...
You shared my gofundme page but didn't make a donation,
Not one single dollar but swear people be hating...
You say we need to stick together,
when the Spotlight is on,
But when the spotlight is gone,
you go back to your ignorance,
Back to that selfish mentality, nigga shit,
Back to that falsehood reality, limited,
Tried to bite my tongue but FUCK IT, I'm militant,
Patting me on my back, like I do it for that...
I do it for the youth,
visit my hood and see proof,
If I didn't have a store you wouldn't see me no more...

A bunch of FB phony's,
time I start revealing,
Put my heart in my city, now I'm all up in my feelings...
If you won't support, cool, but don't act like you do,
A different part of the problem, for those with a clue,
Some gonna smile and say he talented,
but I'm talking to you,
Brain washed by Black-Friday and Christmas too...
Probably lose some friends, but I gotta pick sides,
I'm on the side of the people that are willing to die,
I'm on the side of the ones we lost,
while fighting for-us,
The side of the ones that's lost,
add lighting fluid,
Hope you burn for a long time,
I'm tired of playing,
burn it's a long line,
IJS...

Brain Dead

Monday, why do I have to get up?
Tuesday, this can't be life, WTF!
Wednesday, is hump day, I'm coming around,
Thursday, I'm feeling better, no frown,
Friday, is TURN UP, the weekends here,
Saturday we drank all night,
Sunday, go to church, come home and think all night,
About how you don't want to go to work tomorrow...
It's all a cycle, it's all designed,
Teaching kids to be good workers, instead of fully using their minds,
To start their own...
Go to work, every day, miserable,
Until TGIF is visual,
You have to pay them bills, no residuals,
But you tell yourself, it's all worth it,
Happiness is found in-between the verses,
Seeing life in manuscript, vision it cursive,
Allow me, I'll be your cursor,
If life's a bitch, I'll help you rehearse her,
Things could always be worser...
Yeah, I know that's not a word, but you get my point,
Don't complain about your life, what's the point?
Stop living for the weekend, what's the point?
It's a poem, I'm just speaking, here's my point...
We've been conditioned, to see our condition as a party,
Thinking we going to drink all our pain away,

We hate each other,
While other nationalities love one another,
Working together as sisters and brothers...
Spiritually dead, all we say is quotes,
But we don't live what we say, call that, false hope...
Imprisoned by stinking thinking popping pills and drinking,
Promoting this life style mentally see us shrinking,
We Brain Dead...

Crazy Picker

You have a bad picker,
He just want to stick ya,
Focused on the now,
Can't see the big picture,
Telling all his boys,
That he's going to get with ya,
Telling all your girls,
He might be your next mister...
He saying all the right things,
That you want to hear,
He's wining and dining you,
But Whispers in your ear,
Tell you he's not right,
But you ignore the flags,
Moms don't like him,
And that only make you mad...
You a big girl,
And you make your own decisions,
He's a bad boy,
You proceed, no revisions...
Now you spread those legs,
He don't have protection,
Mentally you said know,
His physical erection,
Got you all ready,
So ya'll do the do,
He's thinking, "now I got this bitch",
You don't have a clue...
9 months later,
Baby number 2,
You was just the side chic,
Everybody knew,
All except for you,

Picking Mr. Wrong,
"Men aint shit",
Yeah, that's your favorite song...
He told you he had 3 kids,
But you aint seen a 1,
You never see his hardships,
All you see is fun...
He dress so nice,
All designer fashions,
He has a nice car,
And he loves it with a passion...
Dudes going to be mad,
I'm telling yall the game,
But some of yall so hard headed,
You going to pick the same,
As you picked the last time,
Expecting different results,
QUEEN, fix your picker,
Until then,
It's your fault...

My People

See somebody getting their ass whipped
You pull out your phone
Never once trying to help though
Other than screaming, SOMEBODY NEEDS TO STOP THEM!!

My people
Get mad when police tell you to disperse
There's nothing to see
But you saw the whole thing
And said, "It has nothing to do with me"

My people
We need to do this or we need to do that
But all you do is talk and don't do anything

My people
How you charge that young man's mother a fee
To work on his game
You got those services for free

My people
We get so mad when another race kill one of us
But when we kill each other
We say, "Free my man, killer"

My people
When you go to department stores
You pay whatever is on the tag
But when you support black owned business
You want an unreasonable discount

My people
When he /she was grinding
You paid them no mind
No support, you even clowned them
But when they blew up
You get mad cause they don't fuck with you..

My people
We complain when it's cold
When it's hot
When it rains
When it's Monday
When you have to work
When you have to pay bills
We find reasons to be unhappy..
But Friday and payday are the happiest days of our lives.

My people
If it don't apply, let it fly
But if any of this applies to you
Change comes from within
I LOVE YOU
Because you're My People

Reinvention

Took a year from the grind,
To strengthen my faith,
Clear up my mind,
Create a new space...
God only knew the struggles ahead,
I had a good plan, but his plan worked instead...
My oldest got better,
More conversations with her sister,
My youngest still finding herself,
My big picture,
Is family business,
As my father would say,
More family visits,
Nelson Avenue, where they stay...
Love keep me going,
Without it I'm done,
The love keeps growing,
Guess I've finally won...
My mindset has changed,
Some thinking's been adjusted,
Some days it feels strange,
But my gut, I can trust it...
Stop smoking weed and cut off a few people,
Scriptures I read,
Show me life as a sequel...
I jumped off a cliff,
Made a collage for a Queen,
Just for her smile,
Unsaid words seen through gleams...
A few disappointments,
But my records expunged,

Raw with no ointment,
The system was lunged,
Right up my ass,
No homo, that's real,
22 years, now I'm free,
That's the deal...
I got some new plans,
Only time will reveal,
Back on my grind,
Not to shine, just to chill,
Pull my girls in tighter,
And together, we'll build,
The rest of my team,
Their identity's sealed...
The Reinvention

Seasons

The pen sits in my hand,
Until my brain commands,
Me to write...
Write what?
So many unfinished thoughts,
Racing around in my head,
Scared...anxious...hopeful...happy,
Impatiently asking
For patience,
As my thoughts now become complacent,
And I struggle for writing substance,
Maybe, I'm afraid of public judgment,
Or maybe,
Its love that eludes me,
I lean on my triangle,
To fill the void,
But the angles are rounding,
Exposing the boy,
The search for joy... in the moment,
My pen becomes still again,
The wind becomes chill again,
Seasons change...

Jumping out the window

Have you ever jumped out of a window?
leap of faith,
don't know what the landing will be,
not trying to save face...
put on my 996 new balance,
landing might be a hard one,
What if she run?
afraid to tell her that I'm feeling her,
might not be reciprocated,
She might not be feeling me that way,
My ego couldn't handle that,
So I hesitated...

Have you ever jumped out of a window?
Followed your heart,
tired of pretending to enjoy smoking weed,
when the high gone I'm mad that I got high...
I want to change,
But that means I'm going to have to cut a few people off,
They're going to think I'm getting soft,
Because I'm partnering with the police,
To increase... The peace... In my community
I want to take some kids on trips,
And I need them pal vans,
The hood is going to look at me funny...

Have you ever jumped out of a window?
seeking your higher self,
on a mission,
No matter what I appear to others,
can't worry about how they see me,
Share my story with youth,
Maybe that will free me...
I realize my seeds are probably going to do greater things than I did,
I welcome that idea,
but my fear,
Is being afraid to be who I am,
Dying, knowing I never reached my full potential,
Crying, because of time wasted, on what was so influential...
Have you ever jumped out of a window?
Have you?
I'll go first...

Everything I See

Phone's silent,
Leaving me alone with my thinking,
Tones of violence,
Racial inequality,
We sinking...
Told my daughter the truth through my perspective,
Open her eyes, she's the future,
Help her see is the objective...
Opportunities come in cycles,
Have to be ready,
Hindsight is so insightful,
Patiently steady...
Pops taught me perseverance,
Nations that fall,
Messengers of interference,
Come to us all...
Signs shown through our dreams,
Showed me a Queen,
Mislead interpretations,
Show me the dean,
Show me unseen,
Truths about this life,
Show me things of my desires delight,
Show me right, but doing wrong,
Feels so right,
Show me light through a song,
Fears take flight...
See the box from the perimeter,
In and out of zones, no limiter,
You start, I'm the finisher,
Listen to a minister, if you want a message,
Join a fraternity, if you need acceptance...
If you want the truth, I'll share it with you,
Reckless,

Starting with myself, let you see my checklist...
Working on insecurities,
Working on my heart,
Working on my selfishness,
That's just to start...
Working on my finances,
Working on my goals,
Working on my characters cons and pros...
Working on the change of who I want to be,
Searching for the good, in everything I see...
Yeah, this is me,
A work still in progress,
Take a look at you, tell me can you digest,
Everything You See?

End of Story

Refuse to succumb to the beating of the drum,
Got us all tuned in to the slum,
Let the beat play...
Things are things, blessings are blessings,
Learned lessons through lack of progression,
Let the heat spray...
Pieces of life injected through a pen,
Reflection from within rejected by evil men,
Followed a path that's been laid by the jinn,
Drop seeds, please let us begin,
Is he anointed?
Big car, big house, big church, big mouth,
Should show you what them offerings about,
You've been exploited...
Promotion on the job but the salary's the same,
Ego puffed up you in charge of the lane,
Can't please them all now they starting to complain,
Pride before the fall cause of thoughts entertained...
Let me get personal,
I shouldn't have let her go,
But that's life you know,
Shorty helped me grow,
Frequent chest pains, my heart is vulnerable,
I guess I'm just, sensitive,
I own it bro...
Got one life to live, don't be scared,
Dream big and take care of your kids,
That's priority...
Earn, don't forget to give, don't be feared,

Can't renege on nothing you did,
Respect authority...
Racial riots,
Black on black crimes, we quiet,
Social networks, addict behaviors,
No step work...
Married but you're cheating,
Cheating your marriage,
Know you should leave,
But you're lacking the courage,
May god forgive us...
No judgment, No court, No jury,
Satin loves it,
Dyeing for fame and glory...
Respect parents,
Childhood and pain runs con-current,
Pops absent,
Equipped with tools, we weren't,
But we made a way,
No complaining today,
Let your actions show after you pray...

Do You See

The start is the finish,
From beginning to end,
Illuminati in our midst,
To sin is to win,
Materialism and greed,
What a devilish grin,
Wolves in sheep's clothing,
Some exposed through a pen...
Watch actions not words,
We so focused on curves,
You don't see her mind,
She could be divine...
You can't see his struggle,
You're blinded by things,
He's a good man,
But you only see bling...
Label chasers!!
Names is the game,
But the clothing's all the same,
They just changed the labels,
Now you going insane...
Trying to get it for Christmas,
What about in July,
Some got it so bad,
They'd watch others die,
Just to get it,
The status
that comes with it,
It's all a facade,
I see all the frauds...

Its only one god,
But religions are many,
Dressed like you rich,
Self-esteem worth a penny...
I'm laughing at life,
Cause I can laugh at myself,
Priorities straight,
Most important is health,
My life is transparent,
But the thinking is stealth,
Chasing dreams with concurrence,
Never chasing the wealth...

Inside Out

Laying in my bed, where my thoughts are centered,
God is there,
so Satan knows he can't enter...
What y'all know about faith when the mortgage is late?
You don't know where the money will come from,
But its food on the plate, cause your kids just ate,
Every month the same fate,
You say you'll do different, all you need is a break,
But you had a few breaks,
it wasn't always so hard,
When your money was right,
you forgot about God,
You say you want change but won't fight for a cause,
but you'll fight for these ignorant ass nigga's and broads...
I take a deep breath,
what thought will come next?
Last night I went home with the person I texted,
It was supposed to be a friendly drink and light conversation,
Ended up at her house,
stemmed from drunken flirtation,
She thanked me in the morning, said I was so giving,
Periodic rendezvous, I disguise it as living...
For real I get bored,
so poems I write,
About life, about death, even about my last night...
Cooked dinner for me and my daughter,
to change the topic,
A waste of my time,
all she eats is hot pockets...
I'm ready to sleep but I'm not finished writing,
I can tell because my mind is still up,

I'm reciting,
through my fingers,
Through ringers, this life has me spinning,
30 days clean, no weed, think I'm winning,
60 more to go, my best friend made the challenge,
90 days is the goal, God please give me balance...
Got 3 salat's in today, tomorrow its 5,
Prayer is essential for those trying to strive,
To be alive is a gift,
to breath is the blessing,
Can't control everything,
so no need for stressing,
About things you can't change,
Now I sound so cliché, what rhymes with cliché?
Ahhh, have a nice day, but its night time,
So I'll say,
she threw the bouquet, but that doesn't make sense,
Now my thoughts are array,
Deeper down on my pillow I sink,
where I'll stay,
Looking up at the tablet, see the point so i jab it,
I'll jab it and jab it,
until you get dizzy,
Few lumps on your head,
my jabs getting busy,
I don't want to knock you out,
just want to wake you up,
Shape you up...
Change is here, its inside out,
As you awake to this change, I'll be asleep,
Hopefully tomorrow we'll be awake at the same time,
That would be powerful...
That would be powerful...

44 Days

The first week was accidental, I was on my grizzy,
2nd week coincidental, God was making me dizzy,
Steady spinning me around, every day was so busy,
By the 3rd week, started analyzing my city...
A Queen said, "Stay strong King, in the end, it's worth it",
My hormones are jumping and I'm questioning my purpose,
This whole abstinence thing, man, this shit for the birds,
But ahhh...I'm trying to fly,
So my thoughts are referred,
Think different to be different,
At least that's what I heard,
My emotions are going crazy,
They're not easily transferred,
More talks with my daughters,
Getting better with words,
Getting better with myself,
Now my thoughts are deferred,
To a greater understanding but the struggles still real,
My homeboy's would laugh so I never reveal,
A few of them on Facebook,
They're respecting my path,
No weed and no sex, they can't even laugh,
Because they know this shit is hard,
Not many can do it,
Every day is a new day,
God help me get through it...

About Last Night

Hidden Feelings

Something's been hiding inside me,
Some days I feel great,
Like I see everything clear,
Gods plan and my role in the plan,
100% content in the moment...
Other days I need stimulation,
From the world outside,
Alcohol, sex, even a conversation...
Sometimes it feels like I can't cope,
I use to smoke weed,
To silence all the racing thoughts in my head,
But that became an expensive coping skill...
Then it was sex,
But I couldn't handle the aftermath,
Giving so much of myself emotionally,
For one climatic moment,
Well, maybe 2 on a good night...

Something's been hiding inside me,
I thought it might be money related,
So I went and got another job,
Now looking for a third,
Maybe I can fill all my time paper chasing,
Once my stacks is up,
That'll surely make me feel better,
Right?
I smile at the people who suggest I pray,
Because that's a given for me...
I was born into favor...
Born into a godly foundation...
With that being said,

My relationship with god is a lifetime journey,
The destination will be revealed in the next life,
Then...a new life begins...

Something's been hiding inside me,
Figured I'd keep shinning a light on it,
For the world to see,
Until the feeling is completely exposed,
Until it can hide no more...

Honesty

I don't want a girlfriend,
Well, that's not quite true,
Truth of the matter is I just don't want you...
That may seem harsh but honesty is best,
Who has time for unnecessary stress?
I know how it feels to be on both ends,
To long for a person that just wants to be friends,
Or to be friends with a person that you're sexing galore,
Now feelings get involved and that person wants more...
Maybe you both had a mutual understanding,
No strings attached, in the moment, no planning,
But more and more moments leads to a thing,
Now your eyes glancing over at their phone, when it rings...
Your mad at yourself because hurt feelings sting,
Said you wouldn't get caught up, this was only a fling...
We all chasing feelings hoping for that stick,
That fairytale love, something more than good dick..
More than good pussy, someone to push me,
Without you even knowing, now you acting all mushy...
We give of ourselves hoping he/she is the one,
When it doesn't work out, we lie and say it was fun,
While it lasted,
When voids are filled, feels fantastic,
But can you be alone with yourself?
I have to ask it...
Can you like somebody without having sex?
Can you stay in the moment without wondering what's next?
Can you let your guards down?
Or are you afraid?
Can you reveal your scars now?
Are your responses delayed?

Can you go against the image you have in your head?
Can't help who you fall in love with,
Does that make you scared?
Stop being safe, standing in place,
Lying next to a person every night, that you hate,
To look in their face,
But you continue to waste...time.
Life is too short to waste time,
I'd rather be alone than waste mine...

If I Share This

If I share this with you,
What perception will you have of me?

I think of you most mornings,
Suppressing those thoughts for fear of losing control,
Though I've already lost control...
Sometimes I say too much,
and I can tell by your response your turned off,
I stop talking,
Anxiously anticipating another day,
To start a new conversation...
I wait patiently,
Then you text me,
"Good morning King, hope you have a great day,"
I smile, you've just made my morning and its only 8:30am,
I'm high, I'm euphoric...
If I share this with you,
What perception will you have of me?

I know I'm not quite your type,
That fact alone humbles my ego,
So many women to pick from,
Woman that could never get past the heartless wall I've created,
My emotions are unavailable to them,
I give bits and pieces of myself to a selected few,
But nobody can have all of me...
I'm afraid to fully let my heart love someone,
I'm afraid of the pain felt when it inevitably comes to an end,
So I defend, my vulnerable heart,
No one can enter...
Then I saw you in my dreams and I knew you had the key,
I knew I would find myself nakedly expressing my thoughts and feelings
for you,

I knew I had to let go of my fake bravado of not wanting a relationship,
I knew you would shatter my (now) glass wall that I carefully tinted,
So no one could see me...
If I share this with you,
What perception will you have of me?

If you're uncomfortable, you'll withdraw,
So I intentionally find a balance between sharing how I feel about you,
And general conversation...
In the beginning, I couldn't handle having a friend that I'm insanely
attracted to,
I wanted more but you wouldn't allow it,
You still don't...
It would've been much easier (for me) to just never call again,
That way, I wouldn't have to feel rejected,
Clearly my thinking needed some adjustments,
Why do I always have to know what's next...
Honestly, even if you chose another,
I would be happy for you as long as you're happy...
But I would always wonder what could have been...
If I share this with you,
What perception will you have of me?

I can imagine us lying in bed on top of the covers,
Talking, listening, laughing,
You, telling me about your day and the annoying lady in your office,
Telling me about your vision for the salon,
I give suggestions here and there,
You're receptive to my suggestions because you believe in me,
You believe in who I am and what I stand for,
And you support it...

I can imagine you trusting me with your heart,
You only know one way to love and I would never let that love down,
I would always be there when you needed me,
And when you don't need me,
I'd be your biggest supporter...
I can imagine you fixing dinner for me,
And sometimes (because my schedule is so flexible), I have dinner pre-
pared before you get home...
I imagine waking up next to you totally loosing myself in the moment,
The moment of looking into your smooth brown skinned, naturally
beautiful, sleep induced face,
Thinking to myself, Wow, this is my Queen,
Touching you gently to pull you closer to me,
You open your eyes and say, "Good morning King",
We both smile, I squeeze you tighter,
We fit like a puzzle,
The imagery is so vivid, so real...
If I share this with you,
What perception will you have of me?

Booty Call

I wish I had a booty call, I'd call her right now,
No strings attached, opposites attract,
I'd even drive across town...
Hate when I get lonely, cause then I start texting,
People that I usually wouldn't,
My hormones want sexing...
You ever text somebody and said some stupid shit?
Then you read over what you sent and feel like an idiot...
I wish somebody text me and say they coming over,
Keep staring at my phone, it doesn't ring,
My house feels colder...
I started to go to a bar and people watch a bit,
Order some shrimp, a long island ice tea,
Post up with my click...
Only problem is, I never really wanted to go,
I just get bored,
Come back home to the same scenario...
This is not a cry for help and I don't want a girl,
I just want a booty call,
To come through and rock my world...

The Art of Casual Sex

I just want casual sex,
But it has to be intimate,
She wants to know what's next,
I just want her to be into it,
I don't know what's next, I'm into this moment,
Renting space in her mind, to decide if I'll own it...
She said, "We must end this, because feelings involved,"
When feelings get high, she's afraid of the fall,
In the past, when she fell,
There was no one to catch her,
I tried to convince her,
But it sounded like lecture...
She liked casual sex, just not with me,
Because we talked about things that our eyes can't yet see,
We talked about dreams and what she aspires to be,
I listened, and I loved, what she inspires in me...
Should I be a jerk?
To have sex unattached,
A little intimacy now and then,
Is that too much to ask?
She said I can't have her body and her mind too,
"Dawood, you have to choose, or I'll choose for you,"
I said, "Well then you choose"
So she chose with her smarts,
I didn't like her choice,
But she protected her heart,
I respect her decision, so I'm playing my part,
I see the big picture now,
A friendship work of art...

Her

Scarred by past love, so rudely interrupted,
Found god through her pain, her heart legally abducted...
So cautious, so strong,
Yet, still insecure,
So beautiful, so sure, she hungers for more,
Of god's grace...
Through her walk, I can tell she's mature,
Far beyond her years,
So far beyond her peers,
I can see in her strength, some of her fears,
I'll be her biggest fan, from the sidelines I'll cheer...
I'm still learning how to "Be,"
So I stay at a distance,
Not sure how she sees me
but I show her consistence...
Caramel skin, short hair, natural beauty, unique,
First met her by chance, appearance petite in my boutique...
She knew my little brother,
My homeboy's cousin is her mother,
Baltimore is so small,
Yet, we never met each other...
I can honestly say it wasn't love at first sight,
Just another valued customer on a late Saturday night...
Saw her a few other times, can't say I felt sparks,
I noticed she was attractive but no flirty remarks,
My responses are pro-active,
Business man, I've embarked,
Sending occasional inbox messages to customers,
Just to talk...
One day she in boxed me,
Felt unusual at first,
For her to reach out, I knew it wasn't to flirt...

It was well wishes and positive energy,
From then on became synergy,
Exchanging musical taste and our philosophical imagery...
This went on for a while,
Normal conversations, nothing deep,
We talked everyday for a couple of weeks...
One night I had a dream about death, made me weak,
My daughters died in my dream, feels too real,
Hope I'm sleep...
This Queen was there with me and I didn't understand,
I hardly even knew her,
Is she part of the plan?
So I went with my gut and asked for a date,
She kindly said, "No, I'm not in that space,"
My ego said, "YO, you don't have to wait,
It's plenty of other women that would love to partake"...
But this Queen, she seemed different,
Running a whole other race...
This Queen, she's indifferent,
Forced me to change pace...
I decided I'd court her, just for the fun,
Just for her smile, just in case she's the one...
She's so nonchalant but I can tell that she likes me,
I'm cool with just friends, anything else seems unlikely...
But the more we talk, the more I seem to like her,
Asking probing questions to find things that will excite her...
I try to fall back and not call as much,
Suppressing my thoughts of me wanting her touch,
In my hands, on my face, on my head, on my chest,
Me touching her too, as we lay down to rest...
I want to be the last person she see,
Every night and every morning,
She wakes up to me,

For the rest of her life,
I can't even lie,
That's a big step,
But I'd give it a try,
For "HER"

I Want Her to Love Me

I want her to love me,
So I spend endless hours on the phone with her,
Texting throughout the day, in-between daily tasks,
Sending occasional selfies, hoping she sends one back,
She does, I smile, we're getting somewhere,
She's becoming comfortable with me,
She begins to feel safe in our conversations,
Opening up about everything,
Past love, family, dreams, disappointments,
And even her sex life and/or lack thereof is freely discussed..

I want her to love me,
So I share my dreams with her,
Tell her some of my disappointments as well,
While still trying to remain a mystery,
Women love mysterious men...
I tell her that I'm a pleaser sexually,
And in that moment (of her highest pleasure) I feel most powerful,
She wants me to feel powerful,
But more than that, she wants to feel pleased,
She wants to feel appreciated..

I want her to love me,
So we mentally fore-play for weeks over the phone,
She tells me her likes and dislikes,
She tells me her sexual frustrations,
I take notes, paying particular attention to every detail...
I'm a perfectionist, I need to successfully please her so well,
That she smiles and may even become wet at the thought/sight of me...
I'm very forward when I see her, yet I'm nonchalant...
I want her to feel like she's in complete control of whatever we're doing,
Until we start doing it, then I'll assume control...

I want her to love me,
Even though I know there's no chance of us spending our life together,
The most we'll ever have is a true friendship with memories of great
sex...
We'll be exclusive friends for awhile,
Until my attention fades or I feel I have nothing more to offer her,
Usually by that point, feelings are involved,
This is when I become contradicting,
My feelings become conflicting,
The one thing I'm sure of is this,
When the dance inevitably comes to an end,
And we no longer talk every day, no more selfies,
No more midday sex dates, not even a morning hello,
When all those things are non-existent,
I still want her to love me
Is that so crazy??

She Came

We talked and laughed about our day,
the book im reading,
the part she play,
rubbing my temple,
in her bed as we lay,
she's one of my best friends,
i have to say...
There's boundaries on, how far we can go
it sucks at times, but we both know,
acceptance is key,
so we both can still grow,
or maybe the boundaries,
is just my ego...
Conversation is dulling,
she's pressed up against me,
her back on my chest,
on our sides, this is simply,
spooning or cuddling,
I'm a sucker for intimacy,
intellect and passion,
two things that interest me...
she pressing against me harder,
i touch the smalls of her back,
she jumps and she shakes,
I feel like a mack!
I slide down her panties,
then press up against her,
sliding my fingers down her body,
i convince her,
that's she's safe...
in this moment, she's safe...
no worries...

I lay in between her,
she's shaking again,
who would have thunk it,
my fucking best friend!
i whisper to her,
"I'm about to go in"
she says "OK",
then we begin...
I'm gentle, she's tense,
so I'm gentle some more,
I pull out, I've decided,
my mouth will explore,
Now she's going crazy,
I go in again,
she's reaching her climax,
my fucking best friend!!
Her toes start to curl,
i can feel on my back,
i tell her "I'm hers" in this moment,
that's fact...
i give her my all,
100□!!
"Can I cum, can I cum",
she gives her consent...
Her foot caught a cramp,
from the pressure I guess,
we both started laughing,
layed back down to rest...
The passion!! The moment!!
Can't be replayed,
until the next time,
now the foundation is layed...
Because She Came

The kind I Want

I want a woman that wakes up Sunday morning looking the same as
she did Saturday night,
A woman who puts her hair in a ponytail and invites me to play fight...
Goes to the market in sweats and sneakers,
Philosophical conversations, she can take my thoughts deeper...
A mother first and foremost but she's freaky when the kids aint watch-
ing,
With my friends, she's the best host, letting me know who she thinks is
plotting...
Maybe this woman doesn't exist and I have unrealistic expectations,
But it's hard for me to settle for a woman with limitations...
She listens to my logic, sometimes implementing my suggestions,
She gives my heart deposits, of blind love with fierce aggression...
She greets me with, "Hey Handsome" stroking my ego ever so gently,
When she stares at me, the world is right, her eyes have just convinced
me,
Simply, that she's in love with me,
But I love her more, not consequently,
We talk and laugh for hours
I share my dreams, she listens intently...
She love my daughters, that's important because my daughters need
that love,
Provides some order, no endorsement, of my past, I was a thug...
She pushes me towards my better self and checks me on the way,
A balance of power and submissiveness, she listens to what I say...
She love when we make love, she whispers in my ear,
"Dawod you are my King and I'm so happy that you're here"...
My ego is a rocket ship, BLAST OFF when I hear that!
She BLASTS OFF too, another world we've traveled, passing stars,
Now were back...

Small Moments

11-7 shift, second phase of my plan,
3rd phase to get paid, another store with my man...
Reached out to a Queen and she cooked me a meal,
Where we go from there only time will reveal...
I stay in the moment, keep my ego in check,
My lane is the grain that's been formed through respect...
This game, I maintain until I can do better,
The rain heels my pain, so the storm is good weather...
Now that's perspective,
To be objective,
When everyone's thinking is so selective,
And reflective,
Of what their eyes see physically...
But it's the third eye that see's quizzically...
But that's too deep;
Had this lady in my sheets, her climax was peaked,
But she stop calling my phone for fears of being alone,
That's a reach...
She was supposed to be my PYT,
But instead it was her that was using me,
I feel cheap...
You get to a point where you're turning down sex,
Unless, it involves intimacy,
If she's interesting to me,
I'll partake in a sexual fantasy,
Even romantically,
If the conversation is emphatically without gravity,
And I can tell she enjoys having me,
Just for that "Small Moment"...

Stuck in My Ways

I get so stuck in my ways sometimes,
Causing my happiness to be delayed sometimes,
I'm so focused on getting paid sometimes,
That I stray from God's path that's laid sometimes...
When it's time for pain, that's all mine,
Trying to mend a broken heart, that takes time,
Change is constant, timing is everything,
If your timing is a little off,
you could possibly lose everything...
I lost a lot in the past 3 weeks,
Shorty had my back when shit wasn't sweet,
Her refrigerator was full of foods that I like to eat,
Now I feel like the fools that I see in the streets,
Who didn't know what they had until it was gone,
Who think they're living right but really they're living wrong...
I should've seen the adjustments I needed to make,
Instead, my foolish pride wouldn't allow me to take,
A good look at the picture,
Ahhh man, I was fake,
Pretending to not care just so I could save face...
Laughing with my friends like it don't really hurt,
When everybody is gone, I feel like the jerk,
Shorty moved on now I'm left with a smirk,
If only I had just put in a little more work...
Now I must wait for an unseen fate,
Nothing like being hungry when there's food on the plate,
Starving for love and now it's a memory,
I had a good girl, she was quite into me,
Now I have to deal with myself,
I'm the enemy,
She was a few years younger but I thought we had chemistry,

Writing poems on Facebook and YouTube for energy...
Afraid to fall in love because I knew it would hurt,
When it's time for the breakup, never thought it would work,
For a minute I believed, she had me wide open,
Young Italian Queen, I started hoping,
That she would be my wife when my money got right,
Couple more kids, full part of my life,
All of a sudden one day, she saw the light,
Decided that I wasn't worth another fight...
I kept the poker face tried to bow out gracefully,
Knowing I had a few other broads that was chasing me,
But my stomach felt funny, a familiar taste to me,
All I could think about was another replacing me...
Celebrating her birthdays giving valentines gifts,
Things I didn't do, our beliefs was split,
She was Catholic, I'm Muslim and it just didn't fit,
But I really loved shorty, man that shit was legit...
If I could do it all over, I'd change a few things,
Communicate better, shop for a ring,
Sometimes what's best might feel real strange,
Go with the flow and think long range...
Try not to get stuck in your ways sometimes,
It can cause your happiness to get delayed sometimes...

Time Appointed

Dealing with shorty for 12 Months on some light shit,
Knowing she would never be the one I'd spend my life wit,
Cause I be on some trife shit,
Early morning late night shit,
Even married chicks come for the dick...
She could never understand that,
Because she fell in love with me,
I tried to turn her off by acting all retardedly,
That never works,
truthfully she stole a part of me,
Jewish chick, 31, she learned to bond with me..
I ain't prejudice about pussy but I'm a sinner,
Pickier than I used to be,
Most of my picks be winners,
I might spend the night and we laugh while eating dinner,
She might start an argument then my patience get thinner,
Roll out,
don't call for a couple of days,
been so long since I let my heart out of the cage,
Guess I'm stuck in my ways,
Probably why I'm still single,
She wants to be with me though,
She hates it when I mingle...
She wants to keep doing what we doing,
I wanna stop cause I ain't growing,
You ever took a big bite out of somebodys life and stop chewing?
Can't swallow the truth,
so the lies start brewing,
Telling myself she just a friend I'm having sex with,
We fallen too deep, can't peep,

I'm on some next shit...
But my next shit is deeper than sex,
She don't believe me when I tell her, "ain't nobody got next"....
I'm just tired of all MY bullshit,
Fake self righteousness,
Everything I write is the truth,
that's why yall liking it,
So you can't point the finger and say men and shit,
now and then I get some pity,
I don't need that shit!
All I need is an outlet for my thoughtfulness wit,
All I need is opportunity to stack some more chips,
My oldest moved back home,
And I've noticed a shift,
with my youngest,
They bonding, it must be a gift...
Got my ebt card today, don't judge me,
Fridge on fleek,
everybody eating lovely,
Now back to shorty,
When we talk, she all bubbly,
I'm hurting inside,
cause the reality is ugly...
I gotta stop sexing her,
Gotta stop texting her,
She keep on telling me,
how I'm bringing out the best in her,
How I should invest in her,
My homies think it's funny,
Saying I gotta a Becky,
But my Becky come from money...
I don't want none of it,
I just like to shut them up,

She ask me why I'm doing this,
I say, cause I don't give a fuck...
That's just my defense,
Everytime a woman gets close,
She gets cut from edges of my fences,
Most of it's senseless,
I just need to find myself,
Listening to Joe Buttons,
Suddenly I find myself,
Writing thoughts on my FB page,
Even though it feels like therapy,
I know it's a stage...
She will make someone a real good wife,
I don't want to be the person in the way,
When that's offered in life,
Everything has a term,
Look for the silver lining,
If you don't, 5 years later you still crying...
Lessons

Acknowledgements

This book is a 4-5 year accumulation of poetry. The poems are about Love, War, Spiritual War, Emotional Insecurities, Triumph, Anger, Responsibility, Fatherhood, motherhood, Society, Protest, Happiness, Romance, Religion, Death, and Life in general. Short stories are told through witty and clever rhymes.

The Author

Dawood Thomas was born in Baltimore, Maryland. He earned his AA Degree at Baltimore city community college in General studies. He is the founder of MFP (My Fathers Plan) which is a non-profit organization designed to target and empower youth through community activism; He is also vice- President of the Pen Lucy Neighborhood Association. This is his first published book. He says, "My daughters are my biggest inspirations".